WHY DO ANIMALS HAVE

TAILS

Elizabeth Miles

Heinemann
LIBRARY

www.heinemann.co.uk/library
Visit our website to find out more information about **Heinemann Library** books.

To order:
 Phone 44 (0) 1865 888066
 Send a fax to 44 (0) 1865 314091
 Visit the Heinemann Bookshop at www.heinemann.co.uk/library to browse our catalogue and order online.

First published in Great Britain by Heinemann Library, Halley Court, Jordan Hill, Oxford OX2 8EJ, a division of Reed Educational and Professional Publishing Ltd. Heinemann is a registered trademark of Reed Educational & Professional Publishing Limited.

OXFORD MELBOURNE AUCKLAND JOHANNESBURG BLANTYRE GABORONE IBADAN PORTSMOUTH NH (USA) CHICAGO

Designed by David Oakley@Arnos Design
Originated by Dot Gradations
Printed in Hong Kong.

ISBN 0 431 15313 2
06 05 04 03 02
10 9 8 7 6 5 4 3 2 1

British Library Cataloguing in Publication Data

Miles, Elizabeth
  Why do animals have tails
  1.Tail - Juvenile literature 2.Physiology - Juvenile literature
  I.Title
  573.9'98'1

Acknowledgements
The Publishers would like to thank the following for permission to reproduce photographs: BBC Natural History Unit/Dan Burton p. 25; BBC Natural History Unit/Phil Savoie p. 26; BBC Natural History Unit/Peter Scoones p. 20; BBC Natural History Unit/Colin Seddon p. 7; BBC Natural History Unit/Mike Wilkes p. 5; Bruce Coleman Collection/Robert Maier p. 10; Bruce Coleman Collection/Hans Reinhard p. 27; Bruce Coleman Collection/Jorg & Petra Wegner p. 8; Corbis pp. 21, 23; Corbis/Joe McDonald pp. 15, 18; digital vision pp. 4, 22, 30; ImageState p. 28; NHPA/Anthony Bannister p. 24; NHPA/Stephen Dalton p. 12; NHPA/Daniel Heuclin p. 29; NHPA/Gerard Lacz pp. 14, 19; NHPA/Christopher Ratier p. 6; Oxford Scientific Films/Clive Bromhall p. 9; Oxford Scientific Films/Mickey Gibson p. 13; Oxford scientific films/Richard Herrmann p. 16; SPL p. 11; Stone p. 17.

Cover photograph reproduced with permission of FPLA.

Our thanks to Claire Robinson, Head of Visitor Information and Education at London Zoo, for her help in the preparation of this book.

Every effort has been made to contact copyright holders of any material reproduced in this book. Any omissions will be rectified in subsequent printings if notice is given to the Publisher.

Contents

Words in bold, **like this**, are explained in the Glossary.

All kinds of tails

Lots of animals have a tail. Some tails are short and some are long, some are narrow and some are wide. A chameleon's tail is quite long and its tip is narrow.

Animal tails may be straight, curved or curly. They can be covered in skin, **scales**, hair or fur. Birds' tails are made of feathers. A woodpecker's stiff tail helps to **support** its body against a tree as it feeds.

Why do animals have tails?

Many animals use their tails for **balance**. As a cheetah chases its **prey**, it stretches out its tail. This helps the cheetah to keep its balance as it twists and turns.

The tiny harvest mouse uses its tail like a safety rope. As it climbs, it curls its tail tightly round a stalk. Like many other animals, harvest mice use their tails for **support**.

Grasping tails

Some animals use their tails like a fifth **limb**. A spider monkey's tail can **grasp** a branch as tightly as a hand. This helps the spider monkey swing through the tree-tops.

A seahorse uses its tail like an **anchor**. It curls its tail tightly round a piece of seaweed. Once it is safely attached, the seahorse will not drift away in the moving water.

Bushy tails

Pine martens live in forests. They run along narrow tree branches, chasing squirrels. A pine marten's long, bushy tail helps it to **balance** so it does not fall.

A squirrel uses its long, bushy tail for balance, too. Its tail is also useful when it sleeps. The squirrel curls up and wraps its tail round its body for extra warmth.

Broad tails

Some squirrels fly from branch to branch. Flying squirrels have flaps of skin between their front and back legs, and a broad tail. They use their flat and wide tail to **steer**.

Beavers have a broad tail, too. They move
their tail up and down to push them through
the water. They also use their tail to **steer**
as they swim.

Tails for hopping

When a kangaroo jumps, its strong tail moves up and down to help it keep its **balance**. When a kangaroo stands still, its stiff tail helps to keep its body upright.

Like the kangaroo, the desert jerboa has very short front legs. It needs its long, **tufted** tail to help it balance. The jerboa also uses its tail to **steer** as it jumps.

Tails for swimming

Most fish have strong upright tails called tail fins. A fish moves its tail fin from side to side, and curves its body at the same time. These movements help fish like these tuna to swim.

A whale is a **mammal** that lives under water. Its tail is wide and lies flat. It moves its tail up and down to swim. Its tail is so powerful, the whale can use it to leap out of the water.

Tails for flying

Birds use their tail to help them in different ways as they fly. A swallow-tailed kite hardly ever flaps its wings. Instead, it **glides** through the air using its tail to **steer**.

When a bird lands, it needs to slow down
quickly. It must **brake**, like an aircraft landing
on a runway. To do this, many birds spread
out their tail feathers, just like this hawk.

Thick tails

Alligators are strong **reptiles** that live in **swamps** and rivers. They have a thick, powerful tail. They sweep their tail from side to side to swim.

A strong, thick tail can be a useful weapon.
If an enemy tries to attack, a Komodo
dragon **thrashes** its tail from side to side.
Its powerful tail frightens the enemy away.

Thin tails

Many animals have a thin tail. Their tail is not very strong, but it can be useful. A zebra can swing its thin, hairy tail to keep flies away.

Elephants are very large animals but they only have a small, thin tail. A baby elephant sometimes holds its mother's tail as they walk along.

Stinging tails

Some tails are dangerous. A desert scorpion has a sting in the tip of its tail. It uses the sting to **inject** poison into any animal that attacks it, or to kill its **prey**.

The stingray is a fish with a deadly tail. If it
is attacked, it lashes its tail from side to side.
Two sharp spines at the base of the tail
inject poison into the attacker.

Fancy tails

Some birds' tails are very colourful. The **male** bird of paradise sometimes shows off its colourful tail feathers by hanging upside down. It is trying to attract a **female** bird.

A male peacock lifts its colourful feathers to attract a female. This fan of special feathers is like a tail. Each feather has a pattern that looks like an eye.

Tails for talking

A dog's tail often shows how the dog is feeling. A wagging tail means the dog is excited. When its tail is down between its legs, the dog is frightened or unhappy.

Some animals use their tail to tell other animals to stay away. When a rattlesnake shakes its tail, it makes a rattling noise. This is a warning not to come closer.

Fact file

- Some animals lose their tail as they grow. A tadpole has a tail for swimming in the water. When it grows into a frog, its tail gradually disappears.

- Ring-tailed lemurs wave their tails like flags so that they can be seen by other lemurs.

- Some lizards have tails that will grow back! When an attacker bites the tail, it breaks off. The lizard escapes and its tail grows back.

This red squirel is using its tail to **balance** as it eats.

Glossary

anchor   heavy object, used to stop a ship from drifting on the sea

balance   keep upright and not fall over

brake   stop suddenly

female   a female parent is the mother

glide   move smoothly through the air

grasp   hold tightly onto something

inject   squirt liquid into something using a sharp point or needle

limb   leg or arm

male   a male parent is the father

mammal   animals that feed their babies with the mother's milk. People are mammals.

prey   animals hunted as food

reptile   animal with hard dry scales on its body

scales   hard skin coverings

steer   guide in different directions

support   help keep an animal in place

swamp   ground where there is lots of water

thrash   move quickly from side to side

tufted   tail with hair or fur at its tip

Index

Titles in the *Why Do Animals Have* series include:

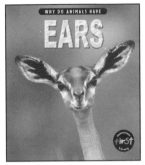

Hardback 0431 15311 6

Hardback 0431 15310 8

Hardback 0431 15326 4

Hardback 0431 15323 X

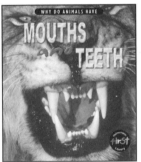

Hardback 0431 15314 0

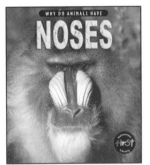

Hardback 0431 15312 4

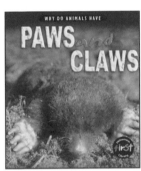

Hardback 0431 15322 1

Hardback 0431 15325 6

Hardback 0431 15313 2

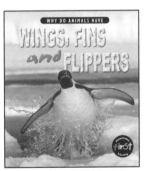

Hardback 0431 15324 8

Find out about the other titles in this series on our website www.heinemann.co.uk/library